CHILDHOOD POEMS

JARROLD POETS SERIES

Also in this series:

Robert and Elizabeth Browning
Robert Burns
Lord Byron
Samuel Taylor Coleridge
John Keats
Rudyard Kipling
The Lady Poets
Scottish Poems & Ballads
Percy Bysshe Shelley
Alfred, Lord Tennyson
The War Poets
William Wordsworth
Animal Poems
Love Poems
Pastoral Poems
Patriotic Poems
Sea Poems

CHILDHOOD POEMS – AN ANTHOLOGY

Poems selected by Joan Forman
Designed by Parke Sutton Publishing Limited
for Jarrold Publishing, Norwich
First published 1994

ISBN 0-7117-0677-8

CONTENTS

JAMES HOGG

A BOY'S SONG

Where the pools are bright and deep,
Where the grey trout lies asleep,
Up the river and o'er the lea,
That's the way for Billy and me.

Where the blackbird sings the latest,
Where the hawthorn blooms the sweetest,
Where the nestlings chirp and flee,
That's the way for Billy and me.

Where the mowers mow the cleanest,
Where the hay lies thick and greenest;
There to trace the homeward bee,
That's the way for Billy and me.

Where the hazel bank is steepest,
Where the shadow falls the deepest,
Where the clustering nuts fall free,
That's the way for Billy and me.

Why the boys should drive away
Little sweet maidens from their play,
Or love to banter and fight so well,
That's the thing I never could tell.

But this I know, I love to play
Through the meadow, among the hay;
Up the water and o'er the lea,
That's the way for Billy and me.

EDWARD LEAR

THE OWL AND THE PUSSY CAT

The Owl and the Pussy cat went to sea
   In a beautiful pea-green boat:
They took some honey, and plenty of money
   Wrapped up in a five-pound note.
The Owl looked up to the stars above,
   And sang to a small guitar,
"O lovely Pussy, O Pussy, my love,
   What a beautiful Pussy you are,
     You are,
     You are!
What a beautiful Pussy you are!"

Pussy said to the Owl, "You elegant fowl,
   How charmingly sweet you sing!
Oh! let us be married; too long we have tarried:
   But what shall we do for a ring?"
They sailed away, for a year and a day
   To the land where the bong-tree grows,

And there in a wood a Piggy-wig stood,
With a ring at the end of his nose,
  His nose,
  His nose,
With a ring at the end of his nose.

"Dear Pig, are you willing to sell for one shilling
  Your ring?" Said the Piggy, "I will."
So they took it away, and were married next day
  By the Turkey who lives on the hill.
They dinèd on mince and slices of quince,
  Which they ate with a runcible spoon,
And hand in hand, on the edge of the sand,
  They danced by the light of the moon,
    The moon,
    The moon,
  They danced by the light of the moon.

JOHN KEATS

LA BELLE DAME SANS MERCI

"O what can ail thee, knight-at-arms,
Alone and palely loitering?
The sedge has wither'd from the lake,
And no birds sing.

"O what can ail thee, knight-at-arms,
So haggard and so woe-begone?
The squirrel's granary is full.
And the harvest's done.

"I see a lily on thy brow
With anguish moist and fever-dew,
And on thy cheeks a fading rose
Fast withereth too."

"I met a lady in the meads,
Full beautiful – a faery's child,
Her hair was long, her foot was light,
And her eyes were wild.

"I made a garland for her head,
And bracelets too, and fragrant zone;
She look'd at me as she did love,
And made sweet moan.

"I set her on my pacing steed
And nothing else saw all day long,
For sidelong would she bend, and sing
A faery's song.

"She found me roots of relish sweet,
And honey wild and manna-dew,
And sure in language strange she said
'I love thee true.'

"She took me to her elfin grot,
And there she wept, and sigh'd full sore,
And there I shut her wild wild eyes
With kisses four.

"And there she lullèd me asleep,
And there I dream'd – Ah! woe betide!
The latest dream I ever dream'd
On the cold hill's side.

"I saw pale kings and princes too,
Pale warriors, death-pale were they all;
They cried – 'La belle Dame sans Merci
Hath thee in thrall!'

"I saw their starved lips in the gloam
With horrid warning gaped wide,
And I awoke and found me here,
On the cold hill's side.

"And this is why I sojourn here
Alone and palely loitering,
Though the sedge is wither'd from the lake
And no birds sing."

RUDYARD KIPLING

THE ROMAN CENTURION'S SONG

Legate, I had the news last night – my cohort ordered home
* By ship to Portus Itius and thence by road to Rome.*
I've marched the companies aboard, the arms are stowed below:
Now let another take my sword. Command me not to go!

I've served in Britain forty years, from Vectis to the Wall.
I have none other home than this, nor any life at all.
Last night I did not understand, but, now the hour draws near
* That calls me to my native land, I feel that land is here.*

Here where men say my name was made, here where my work was done;
Here where my dearest dead are laid – my wife – my wife and son;
Here where time, custom, grief and toil, age, memory, service, love,
Have rooted me in British soil. Ah, how can I remove?

For me this land, that sea, these airs, those folk and fields
*   suffice.*
What purple Southern pomp can match our changeful
*   Northern skies,*
Black with December snows unshed or pearled with
*   August haze –*
The clanging arch of steel-grey March, or June's long-
*   lighted days?*

You'll follow widening Rhodanus till vine and olive lean
Aslant before the sunny breeze that sweeps Nemausus
*   clean*
To Arelate's triple gate; but let me linger on,
Here, where our stiff-necked British oaks confront
*   Euroclydon!*

You'll take the old Aurelian Road through shore-
*   descending pines*
Where, blue as any peacock's neck, the Tyrrhene Ocean
*   shines.*
You'll go where laurel crowns are won, but – will you e'er
*   forget*
The scent of hawthorn in the sun, or bracken in the wet?

Let me work here for Britain's sake – at any task you will –
A marsh to drain, a road to make or native troops to drill.
Some Western camp (I know the Pict) or granite Border keep,
Mid seas of heather derelict, where our old mess-mates sleep.

Legate, I come to you in tears – My cohort ordered home!
I've served in Britain forty years   What should I do in Rome?
Here is my heart, my soul, my mind – the only life I know.
I cannot leave it all behind   Command me not to go!

ROBERT BROWNING

HOW THEY BROUGHT THE GOOD NEWS
FROM GHENT TO AIX

I sprang to the stirrup, and Joris, and he;
I galloped, Dirck galloped, we galloped all three;
"Good speed!" cried the watch, as the gate-bolts undrew;
"Speed!" echoed the wall to us galloping through;
Behind shut the postern, the lights sank to rest,
And into the midnight we galloped abreast.

Not a word to each other; we kept the great pace
Neck by neck, stride by stride, never changing our place;
I turned in my saddle and made its girths tight,
Then shortened each stirrup, and set the pique right,
Rebuckled the cheek-strap, chained slacker the bit,
Nor galloped less steadily Roland a whit.

'T was moonset at starting; but while we drew near
Lokeren, the cocks crew and twilight dawned clear;
At Boom, a great yellow star came out to see;
At Düffeld, 't was morning as plain as could be;

And from Mecheln church-steeple we heard the half-
  chime
So, Jorris broke silence with, "Yet there is time!"

At Aerschot, up leaped of a sudden the sun,
And against him the cattle stood black every one,
To stare thro' the mist at us galloping past,
And I saw my stout galloper Roland at last,
With resolute shoulders, each butting away,
The haze, as some bluff river headland its spray.

And his low head and crest, just one sharp ear bent back
For my voice, and the other pricked out on his track;
And one eye's black intelligence, – ever that glance
O'er its white edge at me, his own master, askance!
And the thick heavy spume-flakes which aye and anon
His fierce lips shook upwards in galloping on.

By Hasselt, Dirck groaned: and cried Joris, "Stay spur!
Your Roos galloped bravely, the fault's not in her,
We'll remember at Aix" – for one heard the quick wheeze
Of her chest, saw the stretched neck and staggering knees,
And sunk tail, and horrible heave of the flank,
As down on her haunches she shuddered and sank.

So, we were left galloping, Joris and I,
Past Looz and past Tongres, no cloud in the sky;
The broad sun above laughed a pitiless laugh,
'Neath our feet broke the brittle bright stubble like chaff;
Till over by Dalhem a dome-spire sprang white,
And "Gallop," gasped Joris, "for Aix is in sight!"

"How they'll greet us!" – and all in a moment his roan
Rolled neck and croup over, lay dead as a stone;
And there was my Roland to bear the whole weight
Of the news which alone could save Aix from her fate,
With his nostrils like pits full of blood to the brim,
And with circles of red for his eye-sockets' rim.

Then I cast loose my buff-coat, each holster let fall,
Shook off both my jack-boots, let go belt and all,
Stood up in the stirrup, leaned, patted his ear,
Called my Roland his pet-name, my horse without peer;
Clapped my hands, laughed and sang, any noise, bad or
*   good,*
Till at length into Aix Roland galloped and stood.

And all I remember is – friends flocking round
As I sat with his head 'twixt my knees on the ground;
And no voice but was praising this Roland of mine,
As I poured down his throat our last measure of wine,
Which (the burgesses voted by common consent)
Was no more than his due who brought good news from
    Ghent.

R. J. YEATMAN AND W. C. SELLAR

HOW I BROUGHT THE GOOD NEWS FROM AIX TO GHENT (OR VICE VERSA)

It runs (or rather gallops) roughly as follows, we quote from memory (having no books of reference at hand) –

I sprang to the rollocks and Jorrocks and me,
And I galloped, you galloped, he galloped, we galloped
   all three . . .
Not a word to each other; we kept changing place,
Neck to neck, back to front, ear to ear, face to face;
And we yelled once or twice, when we heard a clock
   chime,
"Would you kindly oblige us, Is that the right time?"
As I galloped, you galloped, he galloped, we galloped, ye
   galloped, they two shall have galloped; let us trot.

I unsaddled the saddle, unbuckled the bit,
Unshackled the bridle (the thing didn't fit)
And ungalloped, ungalloped, ungalloped, ungalloped a
   bit.

Then I cast off my bluff-coat, let my bowler hat fall,
Took off both my boots and my trousers and all –
Drank off my stirrup-cup, felt a bit tight,
And unbridled the saddle: it still wasn't right.

Then all I remember is, things reeling round
As I sat with my head 'twixt my ears on the ground –
For imagine my shame when they asked what I meant
And I had to confess that I'd been, gone and went
And forgotten the news I was bringing to Ghent,
Though I'd galloped and galloped and galloped and
   galloped and galloped
And galloped and galloped and galloped. (Had I not
   would have been galloped?)

ENVOI

So I sprang to a taxi and shouted "To Aix!"
And he blew on his horn and he threw off his brakes,
And all the way back till my money was spent
We rattled and rattled and rattled and rattled and rattled
And rattled and rattled –
And eventually sent a telegram.

24

Samuel Taylor Coleridge

Kubla Khan

In Xanadu did Kubla Khan
   A stately pleasure-dome decree:
Where Alph, the sacred river, ran
Through caverns measureless to man
   Down to a sunless sea.
So twice five miles of fertile ground
   With walls and towers were girdled round:
And there were gardens bright with sinuous rills
Where blossom'd many an incense-bearing tree;
And here were forests ancient as the hills,
Enfolding sunny spots of greenery.

But O, that deep romantic chasm which slanted
Down the green hill athwart a cedarn cover!
A savage place! as holy and enchanted
As e'er beneath a waning moon was haunted
By woman wailing for her demon-lover!
And from this chasm, with ceaseless turmoil seething,
As if this earth in fast thick pants were breathing,
A mighty fountain momently was forced;

Amid whose swift half-intermitted burst
Huge fragments vaulted like rebounding hail,
Or chaffy grain beneath the thresher's flail:
And 'mid these dancing rocks at once and ever
It flung up momently the sacred river.
Five miles meandering with a mazy motion
Through wood and dale the sacred river ran,
Then reach'd the caverns measureless to man,
And sank in tumult to a lifeless ocean:
And 'mid this tumult Kubla heard from far
Ancestral voices prophesying war!

   The shadow of the dome of pleasure
      Floated midway on the waves;
   Where was heard the mingled measure
      From the fountain and the caves.
It was a miracle of rare device,
A sunny pleasure-dome with caves of ice!

   A damsel with a dulcimer
      In a vision once I saw:
   It was an Abyssinian maid,
      And on her dulcimer she play'd,
   Singing of Mount Abora.

Could I revive within me,
    Her symphony and song,
To such a deep delight 'twould win me,
That with music loud and long,
I would build that dome in air,
That sunny dome! those caves of ice!
And all who heard should see them there,
And all should cry, Beware! Beware!
His flashing eyes, his floating hair!
Weave a circle round him thrice,
    And close your eyes with holy dread,
    For he on honey-dew hath fed,
And drunk the milk of Paradise.

Gerard Manley Hopkins

Spring

Nothing is so beautiful as spring —
  When weeds, in wheels, shoot long and lovely and
    lush;
  Thrush's eggs look little low heavens, and thrush
Through the echoing timber does so rinse and wring
The ear, it strikes like lightnings to hear him sing;
  The glassy peartree leaves and blooms, they brush
  The descending blue; that blue is all in a rush
With richness; the racing lambs too have fair their fling.

Percy Bysshe Shelley

Ozymandias

I met a traveller from an antique land
Who said: Two vast and trunkless legs of stone
Stand in the desert . . . Near them, on the sand,
Half sunk, a shattered visage lies, whose frown,
And wrinkled lip, and sneer of cold command,
Tell that its sculptor well those passions read
Which yet survive, stamped on these lifeless things,
The hand that mocked them, and the heart that fed:
And on the pedestal these words appear:
"My name is Ozymandias, king of kings:
Look on my works, ye Mighty, and despair!"
Nothing beside remains. Round the decay
Of that colossal wreck, boundless and bare
The lone and level sands stretch far away.

Rudyard Kipling

If —

If you can keep your head when all about you
Are losing theirs and blaming it on you,
If you can trust yourself when all men doubt you
But make allowance for their doubting too;
If you can wait and not be tired by waiting,
Or being lied about, don't deal in lies,
Or being hated, don't give way to hating,
And yet don't look too good, nor talk too wise:

If you can dream – and not make dreams your master;
If you can think – and not make thoughts your aim;
If you can meet with Triumph and Disaster
And treat those two imposters just the same;
If you can bear to hear the truth you've spoken
Twisted by knaves to make a trap for fools,
Or watch the things you gave your life to, broken,
And stoop and build 'em up with worn-out tools:

If you can make one heap of all your winnings
And risk it on one turn of pitch-and-toss,
And lose, and start again at your beginnings
And never breathe a word about your loss;
If you can force your heart and nerve and sinew
To serve your turn long after they are gone
And so hold on when there is nothing in you
Except the Will which says to them: "Hold on!"

If you can talk with crowds and keep your virtue,
Or walk with Kings – nor lose the common touch,
If neither foes nor loving friends can hurt you,
If all men count with you, but none too much;
If you can fill the unforgiving minute
With sixty seconds' worth of distance run,
Yours is the Earth and everything that's in it,
And – which is more – you'll be a Man, my son!

A. E. HOUSMAN

FROM: A SHROPSHIRE LAD

When I was one-and-twenty
I heard a wise man say,
"Give crowns and pounds and guineas
But not your heart away;
Give pearls away and rubies
But keep your fancy free."
But I was one-and-twenty,
No use to talk to me.

When I was one-and-twenty
I heard him say again,
"The heart out of the bosom
Was never given in vain;
'Tis paid with sighs a plenty
And sold for endless rue."
And I am two-and-twenty,
And oh, 'tis true, 'tis true.

William Shakespeare

Dirge for Fidele

From: Cymbeline

Fear no more the heat o' the sun,
  Nor the furious winter's rages;
Thou thy worldly task hast done,
  Home art gone, and ta'en thy wages;
Golden lads and girls all must,
As chimney-sweepers, come to dust.

Fear no more the frown o' the great,
  Thou art past the tyrant's stroke:
Care no more to clothe and eat;
  To thee the reed is as the oak:
The sceptre, learning, physic, must
All follow this, and come to dust.

Fear no more the lightning flash,
  Nor the all dreaded thunder-stone;
Fear not slander, censure rash;

Thou hast finish'd joy and moan:
All lovers young, all lovers must
Consign to thee, and come to dust.

No exorciser harm thee!
Nor no witchcraft charm thee!
Ghost unlaid forbear thee!
Nothing ill come near thee!
Quiet consummation have;
And renowned be thy grave.

WILLIAM DAVIES

A GREAT TIME

Sweet Chance, that led my steps abroad,
  Beyond the town, where wild flowers grow –
A rainbow and a cuckoo, Lord!
  How rich and great the times are now!
    Know, all ye sheep
    And cows that keep
On staring that I stand so long
  In grass that's wet from heavy rain –
A rainbow and a cuckoo's song
  May never come together again;
    May never come
    This side the tomb.

JAMES ELROY FLECKER

THE OLD SHIPS

I have seen old ships sail like swans asleep
Beyond the village which men still call Tyre,
With laden age o'ercargoed, dipping deep
For Famagusta and the hidden sun
That rings black Cyprus with a lake of fire;
And all those ships were certainly so old –
Who knows how oft with squat and noisy gun,
Questing brown slaves or Syrian oranges,
The pirate Genoese
Hell-raked them till they rolled
Blood, water, fruit and corpses up the hold?
But now through friendly seas they softly run,
Painted the mid-sea blue or shore-sea green,
Still patterned with the vine and grapes in gold.

But I have seen,
Pointing her shapely shadows from the dawn
An image tumbled on a rose-swept bay,
A drowsy ship of some yet older day;
And, wonder's breath indrawn,

36

Thought I – who knows – who knows – but in that same
(Fished up beyond Æœa, patched up new
– Stern painted brighter blue --)
That talkative, bald-headed seaman came
(Twelve patient comrades sweating at the oar)
From Troy's doom-crimson shore,
And with great lies about his wooden horse
Set the crew laughing, and forgot his course.
It was so old a ship – who knows, who knows?
– And yet so beautiful, I watched in vain
To see the mast burst open with a rose,
And the whole deck put on its leaves again.

ALFRED, LORD TENNYSON

ULYSSES

It little profits that an idle king,
By this still hearth, among these barren crags,
Matched with an agèd wife, I mete and dole
Unequal laws unto a savage race,
That hoard, and sleep, and feed, and know not me.
I cannot rest from travel: I will drink
Life to the lees: all times I have enjoyed
Greatly, have suffered greatly, both with those
That loved me, and alone, on shore, and when
Thro' scudding drifts the rainy Hyades
Vext the dim sea: I am become a name;
For always roaming with a hungry heart
Much have I seen and known; cities of men
And manners, climates, councils, governments,
Myself not least, but honoured of them all;
And drunk delight of battle with my peers,
Far on the ringing plains of windy Troy.
I am a part of all that I have met;
Yet all experience is an arch wherethro'

Gleams that untravelled world, whose margin fades
For ever and for ever when I move.
How dull it is to pause, to make an end,
To rust unburnished, not to shine in use!
As tho' to breathe were life. Life piled on life
Were all too little, and of one to me
Little remains: but every hour is saved
From that eternal silence, something more,
A bringer of new things; and vile it were
For some three suns to store and hoard myself,
And this grey spirit yearning in desire
To follow knowledge like a sinking star,
Beyond the utmost bound of human thought.

    This is my son, mine own Telemachus,
To whom I leave the sceptre and the isle –
Well-loved of me, discerning to fulfil
This labour, by slow prudence to make mild
A rugged people, and thro' soft degrees
Subdue them to the useful and the good.
Most blameless is he, centred in the sphere
Of common duties, decent not to fail
In offices of tenderness, and pay
Meet adoration to my household gods,

When I am gone. He works his work, I mine.
    There lies the port: the vessel puffs her sail:
There gloom the dark broad seas. My mariners,
Souls that have toiled, and wrought, and thought
    with me —
That ever with a frolic welcome took
The thunder and the sunshine, and opposed
Free hearts, free foreheads — you and I are old:
Old age hath yet his honour and his toil;
Death closes all: but something ere the end,
Some work of noble note, may yet be done,
Not unbecoming men that strove with Gods.
The lights begin to twinkle from the rocks:
The long day wanes: the slow moon climbs: the deep
Moans round with many voices. Come, my friends,
'Tis not too late to seek a newer world.
Push off, and sitting well in order smite
The sounding furrows; for my purpose holds
To sail beyond the sunset, and the baths
Of all the western stars, until I die.
It may be that gulfs will wash us down:
It may be we shall touch the Happy Isles,
And see the great Achilles, whom we knew.

Tho' much is taken, much abides; and tho'
We are not now that strength which in old days
Moved earth and heaven; that which we are, we are;
One equal temper of heroic hearts,
Made weak by time and fate, but strong in will
To strive, to seek, to find, and not to yield.

G. K. Chesterton

The Rolling English Road

Before the Roman came to Rye or out to Severn strode,
The rolling English drunkard made the rolling English
  road.
A reeling road, a rolling road, that rambles round the
  shire,
And after him the parson ran, the sexton and the squire;
A merry road, a mazy road, and such as we did tread
The night we went to Birmingham by way of Beachy
  Head.

I knew no harm of Bonaparte and plenty of the Squire,
And for to fight the Frenchman I did not much desire;
But I did bash their baggonets because they came arrayed
To straighten out the crooked road an English drunkard
  made,
Where you and I went down the lane with ale-mugs in
  our hands,
The night we went to Glastonbury by way of Goodwin
  Sands.

His sins they were forgiven him; or why do flowers run
Behind him; and the hedges all strengthening in the sun?
The wild thing went from left to right and knew not
    which was which,
But the wild rose was above him when they found him in
    the ditch.
God pardon us, nor harden us; we did not see so clear
The night we went to Bannockburn by way of Brighton
    Pier.

My friends, we will not go again or ape an ancient rage,
Or stretch the folly of our youth to be the shame of age,
But walk with clearer eyes and ears this path that
    wandereth,
And see undrugged in evening light the decent inn of
    death;
For there is good news yet to hear and fine things to be
    seen,
Before we go to Paradise by way of Kensal Green.

CHARLOTTE BRONTË

SPEAK OF THE NORTH

Speak of the North! A lonely moor
Silent and dark and trackless swells,
The waves of some wild streamlet pour
Hurriedly through its ferny dells.

Profoundly still the twilight air,
Lifeless the landscape; so we deem
Till like a phantom gliding near
A stag bends down to drink the stream.

And far away a mountain zone,
A cold, white waste of snow-drifts lies,
And one star, large and soft and lone,
Silently lights the unclouded skies.

ROBERT LOUIS STEVENSON

IN THE HIGHLANDS

In the highlands, in the country places
Where the old plain men have rosy faces,
And the young fair maidens
Quiet eyes;
Where essential silence cheers and blesses,
And for ever in the hill recesses
Her more lovely music
Broods and dies.

O to mount again where erst I haunted;
Where the old red hills are bird-enchanted,
And the low green meadows
Bright with sward;
And when even dies, the million-tinted,
And the night has come, and planets glinted.
Lo, the valley hollow
Lamp-bestarred!

O to dream, O to awake and wander
There, and with delight to take and render,
Through the trance or silence,
Quiet breath;
Lo! for there, among the flowers and grasses,
Only the mightier movement sounds and passes:
Only winds and rivers,
Life and death.

Sir Walter Scott

Lochinvar

O, Young Lochinvar is come out of the west,
Through all the wide Border his steed was the best;
And save his good broadsword he weapons had none,
He rode all unarm'd, and he rode all alone.
So faithful in love, and so dauntless in war,
There never was knight like the young Lochinvar.

He staid not for brake, and he stopped not for stone,
He swam the Esk river where ford there was none;
But ere he alighted at Netherby gate,
The bride had consented, the gallant came late:
For a laggard in love, and a dastard in war,
Was to wed the fair Ellen of brave Lochinvar.

So boldly he enter'd the Netherby Hall,
Among bride's-men, and kinsmen and brothers, and all:
Then spoke the bride's father, his hand on his sword,
(For the craven bridegroom said never a word),
"O come ye in peace here, or come ye in war,
Or to dance at our bridal, young Lord Lochinvar?"

"I long woo'd your daughter, my suit you denied; —
Love swells like the Solway, but ebbs like its tide —
And now I am come, with this lost love of mine,
To lead but one measure, drink one cup of wine.
There are maidens in Scotland more lovely by far,
That would gladly be bride to young Lochinvar."

The bride kiss'd the goblet: the knight took it up,
He quaff'd of the wine, and he threw down the cup.
She look'd down to blush, and she look'd up to sigh,
With a smile on her lips, and a tear in her eye.
He took the soft hand, ere her mother could bar,
"Now tread we a measure!" said young Lochinvar.

So stately his form, and so lovely her face,
That never a hall such a galliard did grace;
While her mother did fret, and her father did fume,
And the bridegroom stood dangling his bonnet and
    plume,
And the bride-maidens whisper'd, "'Twere better by far,
To have match'd our fair cousin with young
    Lochinvar."

One touch of her hand, and one word in her ear,
When they reached the hall-door and the charger stood
    near;
So light to the croupe the fair lady he swung,
So light to the saddle before her he sprung!
"She is won! we are gone, over bank, bush and scaur;
They'll have fleet steeds that follow," quoth young
    Lochinvar.

There was mounting 'mong Graemes of the Netherby
    clan;
Forsters, Fenwicks, and Musgraves, they rode and they
    ran:
There was racing, and chasing, on Cannobie Lee,
But the lost bride of Netherby ne'er did they see.
So daring in love, and so dauntless in war,
Have ye e'er heard of gallant like young Lochinvar?

HAROLD MONRO

OVERHEARD ON A SALTMARSH

Nymph, nymph, what are your beads?

Green glass, goblin. Why do you stare at them?

Give them me.

        No.

Give them me. Give them me.

           No.

Then I will howl all night in the reeds,
Lie in the mud and howl for them.

Goblin, why do you love them so?

They are better than stars or water,
Better than voices of winds that sing,
Better than any man's fair daughter,
Your green glass beads on a silver ring.

Hush, I stole them out of the moon.

Give me your beads, I want them.

> *No.*

I will howl in a deep lagoon
For your green glass beads, I love them so.
Give them me. Give them me.

> *No.*

JOHN DRINKWATER

MOONLIT APPLES

At the top of house the apples are laid in rows,
And the skylight lets the moonlight in, and those
Apples are deep-sea apples of green. There goes
  A cloud on the moon in the autumn night.

A mouse in the wainscot scratches, and scratches, and
  then
There is no sound at the top of the house of men
Or mice; and the cloud is blown, and the moon again
  Dapples the apples with deep-sea light.

They are lying in rows there, under the gloomy beams;
On the sagging floor; they gather the silver streams
Out of the moon, those moonlit apples of dreams,
  And quiet is the steep stair under.

In the corridors under there is nothing but sleep.
And stiller than ever on orchard boughs they keep
Tryst with the moon, and deep is the silence, deep
  On moon-washed apples of wonder.

LEWIS CARROLL

FATHER WILLIAM

"You are old, Father William," the young man said,
"And your hair has become very white;
And yet you incessantly stand on your head –
Do you think, at your age, it is right?"

"In my youth," Father William replied to his son,
"I feared it might injure the brain;
But now that I'm perfectly sure I have none,
Why, I do it again and again."

"You are old," said the youth, "as I mentioned before,
And have grown most uncommonly fat;
Yet you turned a back somersault in at the door –
Pray, what is the reason of that?"

"In my youth," said the sage, as he shook his grey locks,
"I kept all my limbs very supple
By the use of this ointment – one shilling the box –
Allow me to sell you a couple."

"You are old," said the youth, "and your jaws are too
    weak
For anything tougher than suet;
Yet you finished the goose, with the bones and the beak;
Pray, how did you manage to do it?"

"In my youth," said his father, "I took to the law,
And argued each case with my wife;
And the muscular strength which it gave to my jaw,
Has lasted the rest of my life."

"You are old," said the youth; "one would hardly
    suppose
That your eye was as steady as ever;
Yet you balanced an eel on the end of your nose –
What made you so awfully clever?"

"I've answered three questions, and that is enough,"
Said his father; "don't give yourself airs!
Do you think I can listen all day to such stuff?
Be off, or I'll kick you down-stairs!"

Anonymous

The Two Sisters of Binnorie

There were two sisters sat in a bower;
  Binnorie, O Binnorie;
There came a knight to be their wooer;
  By the bonny mill-dams of Binnorie.

He courted the eldest with gloves and rings,
But he loved the youngest above all things.

The eldest was vexed to despair,
And much she envied her sister fair.

The eldest said to the youngest one,
"Will ye see our father's ships come in?"

She's taken her by the lily-white hand,
And led her down to the river strand.

The youngest stood upon a stone;
The eldest came and pushed her in.

"O sister, sister, reach your hand,
And you shall be heir of half my land.

"O sister, reach me but your glove
And sweet William shall be all your love."

"Sink on, nor hope for hand or glove!
Sweet William shall surely be my love."

Sometimes she sank, sometimes she swam,
Until she came to the mouth of the dam.

Out then came the miller's son
And saw the fair maid swimming in.

"O father, father, draw your dam!
Here's either a mermaid or a swan."

The miller hasted and drew his dam,
And there he found a drowned woman.

You could not see her middle small,
Her girdle was so rich withal.

You could not see her yellow hair
For the gold and pearls that clustered there.

And by there came a harper fine
Who harped to nobles when they dine.

And when he looked that lady on,
He sighed and made a heavy moan.

He's made a harp of her breast bone,
Whose sounds would melt a heart of stone.

He's taken three locks of her yellow hair,
And with them strung his harp so rare.

He went into her father's hall
To play his harp before them all.

But as he laid it on a stone,
The harp began to play alone.

And soon the harp sang loud and clear,
"Farewell, my father and mother dear.

"Farewell, farewell, my brother Hugh,
Farewell, my William, sweet and true."

And then, as plain as plain could be,
    (Binnorie, O Binnorie)
"There sits my sister who drowned me
    By the bonny mill-dams of Binnorie!"

ROBERT LOUIS STEVENSON

THE VAGABOND

Give to me the life I love,
Let the lave go by me,
Give the jolly heaven above
And the by-way nigh me,
Bed in the bush with stars to see,
Bread I dip in the river –
There's the life for a man like me,
There's the life for ever.

Let the blow fall soon or late,
Let what will be o'er me;
Give the face of earth around
And the road before me.
Wealth I seek not, hope nor love,
Nor a friend to know me;
All I seek, the heaven above,
And the road below me.

Or let autumn fall on me
Where afield I linger,
Silencing the bird on tree,
Biting the blue finger,
White as meal the frosty field –
Warm the fireside haven –
Not to autumn will I yield,
Not to winter even!

Let the blow fall soon or late,
Let what will be o'er me;
Give the face of earth around,
And the road before me.
Wealth I ask not, hope nor love,
Nor a friend to know me.
All I ask, the heaven above,
And the road below me.

JOHN KEATS

MEG MERRILIES

Old Meg she was a gipsy;
And lived upon the moors:
Her bed it was the brown heath turf,
And her house was out of doors.
Her apples were swart blackberries,
Her currants, pods o'broom;
Her wine was dew of the wild white rose,
Her book a church-yard tomb.

Her brothers were the craggy hills,
Her sisters larchen trees;
Alone with her great family
She lived as she did please.
No breakfast had she many a morn,
No dinner many a noon,
And 'stead of supper, she would stare
Full hard against the moon.

But every morn, of woodbine fresh
She made her garlanding,
And every night, the dark glen yew
She wove and she would sing.
And with her fingers, old and brown,
She plaited mats of rushes,
And gave them to the cottagers
She met among the bushes.

Old Meg was brave as Margaret Queen,
And tall as Amazon;
An old red blanket cloak she wore,
A chip-hat had she on.
God rest her aged bones somewhere!
She died full long agone!

EDWARD THOMAS

ADLESTROP

Yes. I remember Adlestrop –
The name, because one afternoon
Of heat the express-train drew up there
Unwontedly. It was late June.

The steam hissed. Someone cleared his throat.
No one left and no one came
On the bare platform. What I saw
Was Adlestrop – only the name

And willows, willow-herb, and grass,
And meadowsweet, and haycocks dry,
No whit less still and lonely fair
Than the high cloudlets in the sky.

And for that minute a blackbird sang
Close by, and round him, mistier,
Farther and farther, all the birds
Of Oxfordshire and Gloucestershire.

RUDYARD KIPLING

THE WAY THROUGH THE WOODS

They shut the road through the woods
Seventy years ago.
Weather and rain have undone it again,
And now you would never know
There was once a road through the woods
Before they planted the trees.
It is underneath the coppice and heath,
And the thin anemones.
Only the keeper sees
That, where the ring-dove broods,
And the badgers roll at ease,
There was once a road through the woods.

Yes, if you enter the woods
Of a summer evening late,
When the night-air cools on the trout-ringed pools
Where the otter whistles his mate,

(They fear not men in the woods,
Because they see so few.)
You will hear the beat of a horse's feet,
And the swish of a skirt in the dew,
Steadily cantering through
The misty solitudes,
As though they perfectly knew
The old lost road through the woods . . .
But there is no road through the woods.

ROBERT BROWNING

HOME THOUGHTS, FROM ABROAD

Oh, to be in England
Now that April's there,
And whoever wakes in England
Sees, some morning, unaware,
That the lowest boughs and the brushwood sheaf
Round the elm-tree bole are in tiny leaf,
While the chaffinch sings on the orchard bough,
In England – now!

And after April, when May follows,
And the whitethroat builds, and all the swallows,
Hark! where my blossomed pear-tree in the hedge
Leans to the field and scatters on the clover
Blossoms and dewdrops – at the bent spray's edge –
That's the wise thrush; he sings each song twice over,
Lest you should think he never could recapture
The first fine careless rapture!
And though the fields look rough with hoary dew,
All will be gay when noontide wakes anew
The buttercups, the little children's dower,
– Far brighter than this gaudy melon-flower.

THOMAS CAMPBELL

LORD ULLIN'S DAUGHTER

A Chieftain to the Highlands bound
Cries "Boatman, do not tarry!
And I'll give thee a silver pound
To row us o'er the ferry!

"Now who would be ye, would cross Lochgyle
This dark and stormy water?"
"O I'm the chief of Ulva's isle,
And this, Lord Ullin's daughter.

"And fast before her father's men
Three days we've fled together,
For should he find us in the glen,
My blood would stain the heather.

"His horsemen hard behind us ride –
Should they our steps discover,
Then who would cheer my bonny bride
When they have slain her lover?"

Out spake the hardy Highland wight.
"I'll go, my chief, I'm ready:
It is not for your silver bright,
But for your winsome lady: –

"And by my word! the bonny bird
In danger shall not tarry;
So though the waves are raging white
I'll row you o'er the ferry."

By this the storm grew loud apace,
The water-wraith was shrieking;
And in the scowl of heaven each face
Grew dark as they were speaking.

But still as wilder blew the wind
And as the night grew drearer,
Adown the glen rode armed men,
Their trampling sounded nearer.

"O haste thee, haste!" the lady cries,
"Though tempests round us gather;
I'll meet the raging of the skies,
But not an angry father."

The boat has left a stormy land,
A stormy sea before her, –
When, oh! too strong for human hand
The tempest gather'd o'er her.

And still they row'd amidst the roar
Of waters still prevailing:
Lord Ullin reached that fatal shore, –
His wrath was changed to wailing.

For, sore dismay'd, through storm and shade
His child he did discover: –
One lovely hand she stretch'd for aid,
And one was round her lover.

"Come back! come back!" he cried in grief,
"Across this stormy water:
And I'll forgive your Highland chief,
My daughter! – O my daughter!"

'Twas vain: the loud waves lash'd the shore,
Return or aid preventing:
The waters wild went o'er his child,
And he was left lamenting.

KENNETH GRAHAME
DUCKS' DITTY

All along the backwater,
Through the rushes tall,
Ducks are a-dabbling,
Up tails all!

Ducks' tails, drakes' tails,
Yellow feet a-quiver,
Yellow bills all out of sight
Busy in the river!

Slushy green undergrowth
Where the roach swim –
Here we keep our larder,
Cool and full and dim!

Every one for what he likes!
We like to be
Heads down, tails up,
Dabbling free!

High in the blue above
Swifts whirl and call –
We are down a-dabbling
Up tails all!

Anonymous

The Wraggle Taggle Gipsies

There were three gipsies a-come to my door,
And downstairs ran this a-lady, O!
One sang high, and another sang low,
And the other sang, Bonny, bonny Biscay, O!

Then she pulled off her silk-finished gown
And put on hose of leather, O!
The ragged, ragged rags about our door –
She's gone with the wraggle taggle gipsies, O!

It was late last night, when my lord came home,
Enquiring for his a-lady, O!
The servants said, on every hand:
"She's gone with the wraggle taggle gipsies, O!"

"O saddle to me my milk-white steed.
Go and fetch me my pony, O!
That I may ride and seek my bride,
Who is gone with the wraggle taggle gipsies, O!"

O he rode high and he rode low,
He rode through woods and copses too,
Until he came to an open field,
And there he espied his a-lady, O!

"What makes you leave your house and land?
What makes you leave your money, O?
What makes you leave your new-wedded lord;
To go with the wraggle taggle gipsies, O!"

"What care I for my house and my land?
What care I for my money, O?
What care I for my new-wedded lord?
I'm off with the wraggle taggle gipsies, O!"

"Last night you slept on a goose-feather bed,
With the sheet turned down so bravely, O!
And to-night you'll sleep in a cold open field,
Along with the wraggle taggle gipsies, O!"

"What care I for a goose-feather bed,
With the sheet turned down so bravely, O?
For to-night I shall sleep in a cold open field,
Along with the wraggle taggle gipsies, O!"

ROBERT LOUIS STEVENSON

REQUIEM

Under the wide and starry sky,
Dig the grave and let me lie.
Glad did I live and gladly die,
   And I laid me down with a will.

This be the verse you grave for me:
Here he lies where he longed to be,
Home is the sailor, home from sea,
   And the hunter home from the hill.

Edward Lear

The Jumblies

They went to sea in a sieve, they did,
In a sieve they went to sea:
In spite of all their friends could say,
On a winter's morn, on a stormy day,
In a sieve they went to sea.
And when the sieve turned round and round
And everyone cried, "You'll all be drowned!"
They called aloud "Our sieve ain't big,
But we don't care a button! we don't care a fig!
In a sieve we'll go to sea!"
  Far and few, far and few
  Are the lands where the Jumblies live;
  Their heads are green, and their hands are blue,
  And they went to sea in a sieve.

They sailed away in a sieve, they did,
In a sieve they sailed so fast.
With only a beautiful pea-green veil
Tied with a riband by way of a sail,
To a small tobacco-pipe mast;

And everyone said, who saw them go,
"O, won't they be soon upset, you know!
For the sky is dark, and the voyage is long,
And happen what may, it's extremely wrong
In a sieve to sail so fast!"
    Far and few, far and few
    Are the lands where the Jumblies live;
    Their heads are green, and their hands are blue,
    And they went to sea in a sieve.

The water it soon came in, it did,
The water it soon came in;
So to keep them dry, they wrapped their feet
In a pinky paper all folded neat,
And they fastened it down with a pin.
And they passed the night in a crockery jar,
And each of them said "How wise we are!
Though the sky be dark, and the voyage be long,
Yet we never can think we were rash or wrong,
While round in our sieve we spin!"
    Far and few, far and few
    Are the lands where the Jumblies live;
    Their heads are green, and their hands are blue,
    And they went to sea in a sieve.

And all night long they sailed away;
And when the sun went down,
They whistled and warbled a moony song
To the echoing sound of a coppery gong,
In the shade of the mountains brown.
"O Tinballo! How happy we are,
When we live in a sieve and a crockery jar,
And all night long in the moonlight pale,
We sail away with a pea-green sail
In the shade of the mountains brown!"
　　Far and few, far and few
　　Are the lands where the Jumblies live;
　　Their heads are green, and their hands are blue,
　　And they went to sea in a sieve.

They sailed to the Western Sea they did,
To a land all covered with trees,
And they bought an owl and a useful cart
And a pound of rice and a cranberry tart
And a hive of silvery bees.
And they bought a pig, and some green jack-daws
And a lovely monkey with lollipop paws,
And forty bottles of Ring-Bo-Ree,
And no end of stilton cheese.

Far and few, far and few
Are the lands where the Jumblies live;
Their heads are green, and their hands are blue,
And they went to sea in a sieve.

And in twenty years they all came back,
In twenty years or more,
And everyone said "How tall they've grown!
For they've been to the Lakes, and the Terrible Zone,
And the hills of the Chankley Bore,"
And they drank their health, and gave them a feast
Of dumplings made of beautiful yeast;
And everyone said, "If we only live,
We too will go to sea in a sieve
To the hills of the Chankley Bore."
  Far and few, far and few
  Are the lands where the Jumblies live;
  Their heads are green, and their hands are blue,
  And they went to sea in a sieve.

CHRISTINA ROSSETTI

STONES

An emerald is as green as grass;
A ruby as red as blood;
A sapphire shines as blue as heaven;
A flint lies in the mud.

A diamond is a brilliant stone
To catch the world's desire;
An opal holds a fiery spark;
But a flint holds fire.

Robert Browning

My Last Duchess

Ferrara

That's my last Duchess painted on the wall,
Looking as if she were alive. I call
That piece a wonder, now: Frà Pandolf's hands
Worked busily a day, and there she stands.
Will't please you sit and look at her? I said
"Frà Pandolf" by design, for never read
Strangers like you that pictured countenance,
The depth and passion of its earnest glance,
But to myself they turned (since none puts by
The curtain I have drawn for you, but I)
And seemed as they would ask me, if they durst,
How such a glance came there; so, not the first
Are you to turn and ask thus. Sir, 'twas not
Her husband's presence only, called that spot
Of joy into the Duchess' cheek: perhaps
Frà Pandolf chanced to say "Her mantle laps
Over my lady's wrist too much," or "Paint
Must never hope to reproduce the faint

Half-flush that dies along her throat": such stuff
Was courtesy, she thought, and cause enough
For calling up that spot of joy. She had
A heart — how shall I say? — too soon made glad,
Too easily impressed; she liked whate'er
She looked on, and her looks went everywhere.
Sir, 'twas all one! My favour at her breast,
The dropping of the daylight in the West,
The bough of cherries some officious fool
Broke in the orchard for her, the white mule
She rode with round the terrace — all and each
Would draw from her alike the approving speech,
Or blush, at least. She thanked men, — good! but
      thanked
Somehow — I know not how — as if she ranked
My gift of a nine-hundred-years-old name
With anybody's gift. Who'd stoop to blame
This sort of trifling? Even had you skill
In speech — (which I have not) — to make your will
Quite clear to such an one, and say, "Just this
Or that in you disgusts me; here you miss,
Or there exceed the mark" — and if she let
Herself be lessoned so, nor plainly set
Her wits to yours, forsooth, and made excuse,

– E'en then would be some stooping; and I choose
Never to stoop. Oh sir, she smiled, no doubt,
Whene'er I passed her; but who passed without
Much the same smile? This grew; I gave commands;
Then all smiles stopped together. There she stands
As if alive. Will't please you rise? We'll meet
The company below, then. I repeat,
The Count your master's known munificence
Is ample warrant that no just pretence
Of mine for dowry will be disallowed;
Though his fair daughter's self, as I avowed
At starting, is my object. Nay, we'll go
Together down, sir. Notice Neptune, though,
Taming a sea-horse, thought a rarity,
Which Claus of Innsbruck cast in bronze for me!

EDWARD FITZGERALD

FROM: THE RUBÁIYÁT OF OMAR KHAYYÁM

Awake! for Morning in the Bowl of Night
Has flung the Stone that puts the Stars to Flight:
*   And lo! the Hunter of the East has caught*
The Sultán's Turret in a Noose of Light.

Irám indeed is gone with all its Rose,
And Jamshýd's Sev'n-ring'd Cup where no one knows;
*   But still the Vine her ancient Ruby yields,*
And still a Garden by the Water blows.

Come, fill the Cup, and in the Fire of Spring
The Winter Garment of Repentance fling:
*   The Bird of Time has but a little way*
To fly – and Lo! the Bird is on the Wing.

Here with a Loaf of Bread beneath the Bough,
A Flask of Wine, a Book of Verse – and Thou
*   Beside me singing in the Wilderness –*
And Wilderness is Paradise enow.

Think, in this battered Caravanserai
Whose Doorways are alternate Night and Day,
  How Sultán after Sultán with his Pomp
Abode his Hour or two, and went his way.

I sometimes think that never blows so red
The Rose as where some buried Caesar bled:
  That every Hyacinth the Garden wears
Dropt in its Lap from some once lovely Head.

Ah, my Belovéd, fill the cup that clears
TO-DAY of past Regrets and future Fears –
  To-morrow? – Why, To-morrow I may be
Myself with Yesterday's Sev'n Thousand Years.

Alike for those who for TO-DAY prepare,
And those that after a TO-MORROW stare,
  A Muezzín from the Tower of Darkness cries,
"Fools! your Reward is neither Here nor There!"

Myself when young did eagerly frequent
Doctor and Saint, and heard great Argument
  About it and about, but evermore
Came out by the same Door as in I went.

Ah, fill the Cup: – what boots it to repeat
How time is slipping underneath our Feet:
Unborn To-MORROW and dead YESTERDAY,
Why fret about them if To-DAY be sweet!

The Moving Finger writes; and, having writ,
Moves on; nor all your Piety nor Wit
Shall lure it back to cancel half a line,
Nor all your Tears wash out a word of it.

Ah, with the Grape my fading Life provide,
And wash my Body whence the Life has died,
And in a Winding-sheet of Vine-leaf wrapt,
So bury me by some sweet Garden side.

Alas, that Spring should vanish with the Rose!
That Youth's sweet-scented Manuscript should close!
The Nightingale that in the branches sang,
Ah, whence, and whither flown again, who knows?

Oh Love! could you and I with Fate conspire
To grasp this sorry Scheme of Things entire,
Would not we shatter it to bits – and then
Re-mould it nearer to the Heart's Desire!

WILLIAM ALLINGHAM

THE FAIRIES

Up the airy mountain,
Down the rushy glen,
We daren't go a-hunting
For fear of little men;
Wee folk, good folk,
Trooping all together;
Green jacket, red cap,
And white owl's feather!

Down along the rocky shore
Some make their home,
They live on crispy pancakes
Of yellow-tide foam;
Some in the reeds
Of the black mountain lake,
With frogs for their watch-dogs
All night awake.

High on the hill-top
The old King sits;

He is now so old and grey
He's nigh lost his wits.
With a bridge of white mist
Columbkill he crosses,
On his stately journeys
From Slieveleague to Rosses;
Or going up with music
On cold starry nights,
To sup with the Queen
Of the gay Northern Lights.

They stole little Bridget
For seven years long;
When she came down again
Her friends were all gone.
They took her lightly back,
Between the night and morrow,
They thought that she was fast asleep,
But she was dead with sorrow.
They have kept her ever since.
Deep within the lakes,
On a bed of flag-leaves,
Watching till she wakes.

By the craggy hill-side,
Through the mosses bare,
They have planted thorn-trees
For pleasure here and there.
Is any man so daring
As dig them up in spite,
He shall find their sharpest thorns
In his bed at night.

Up the airy mountain,
Down the rushy glen,
We daren't go a-hunting
For fear of little men;
Wee folk, good folk,
Trooping all together;
Green jacket, red cap,
And white owl's feather!

ANONYMOUS

MATTHEW, MARK, LUKE, AND JOHN

Matthew, Mark, Luke, and John,
Bless the bed that I lie on.
Before I lay me down to sleep
I give my soul to Christ to keep.
Four corners to my bed,
Four angels there aspread,
Two to foot, and two to head,
And four to carry me when I'm dead.

I go by sea, I go by land,
The Lord made me with His right hand.
If any danger come to me,
Sweet Jesus Christ deliver me.
He's the branch and I'm the flower,
Pray God send me a happy hour,
And if I die before I wake,
I pray that Christ my soul will take.

Lord Byron

The Destruction of Sennacherib

The Assyrian came down like the wolf on the fold,
And his cohorts were gleaming in purple and gold;
And the sheen of their spears was like stars on the sea,
When the blue wave rolls nightly on deep Galilee.

Like the leaves of the forest when Summer is green,
That host with their banners at sunset were seen:
Like the leaves of the forest when Autumn hath blown,
That host on the morrow lay wither'd and strown.

For the Angel of Death spread his wings on the blast,
And breathed in the face of the foe as he pass'd;
And the eyes of the sleepers wax'd deadly and chill,
And their hearts but once heaved, and for ever grew still!

And there lay the steed with his nostril all wide,
But through it there roll'd not the breath of his pride;
And the foam of his gasping lay white on the turf,
And cold as the spray of the rock-beating surf.

And there lay the rider distorted and pale,
With the dew on his brow, and the rust on his mail:
And the tents were all silent, the banners alone,
The lances unlifted, the trumpet unblown.

And the widows of Ashur are loud in their wail,
And the idols are broke in the temple of Baal;
And the might of the Gentile, unsmote by the sword,
Hath melted like snow in the glance of the Lord!

ROBERT BROWNING

THE PIED PIPER OF HAMELIN

Hamelin Town's in Brunswick,
By famous Hanover city;
The river Weser, deep and wide,
Washes its wall on the southern side;
A pleasanter spot you never spied;
But, when begins my ditty,
Almost five hundred years ago,
To see the townsfolk suffer so
From vermin was a pity.

Rats!
They fought the dogs, and killed the cats,
And bit the babies in the cradles,
And ate the cheeses out of the vats,
And licked the soup from the cooks' own ladles,
Split open the kegs of salted sprats,
Made nests inside men's Sunday hats,
And even spoiled the women's chats,
By drowning their speaking
With shrieking and squeaking
In fifty different sharps and flats.

At last the people in a body
To the Town Hall came flocking:
"'Tis clear," cried they, "our Mayor's a noddy;
And as for our Corporation – shocking
To think we buy gowns lined with ermine
For dolts that can't or won't determine
What's best to rid us of our vermin!
You hope, because you're old and obese,
To find in the furry civic robe ease?
Rouse up, Sirs! Give your brains a racking
To find the remedy we're lacking,
Or, sure as fate, we'll send you packing!"
At this the Mayor and Corporation
Quaked with a mighty consternation.

An hour they sate in council,
At length the Mayor broke silence:
"For a guilder I'd my ermine gown sell;
I wish I were a mile hence!
It's easy to bid one rack one's brain –
I'm sure my poor head aches again
I've scratched it so, and all in vain.
Oh for a trap, a trap, a trap!"
Just as he said this, what should hap

At the chamber door but a gentle tap?
"Bless us," cried the Mayor, "what's that?"
(With the Corporation as he sat,
Looking little though wondrous fat;
Nor brighter was his eye, nor moister
Than a too-long-opened oyster,
Save when at noon his paunch grew mutinous
For a plate of turtle green and glutinous)
"Only a scraping of shoes on the mat?
Anything like the sound of a rat
Makes my heart go pit-a-pat!"

"Come in!" – the Mayor cried, looking bigger:
And in did come the strangest figure!
His queer long coat from heel to head
Was half of yellow and half of red;
And he himself was tall and thin,
With sharp blue eyes, each like a pin,
And light loose hair, yet swarthy skin,
No tuft on cheek nor beard on chin,
But lips where smiles went out and in –
There was no guessing his kith and kin!
And nobody could enough admire
The tall man and his quaint attire:

Quoth one: "It's as my great-grandsire,
Starting up at the Trump of Doom's tone,
Had walked this way from his painted tomb-stone!"

He advanced to the council-table:
And, "Please your honours," said he, "I'm able
By means of a secret charm to draw
All creatures living beneath the sun,
That creep or swim or fly or run,
After me so as you never saw!
And I chiefly use my charm
On creatures that do people harm,
The mole and toad and newt and viper;
And people call me the Pied Piper."
(And here they noticed round his neck
A scarf of red and yellow stripe,
To match with his coat of the self-same cheque;
And at the scarf's end hung a pipe;
And his fingers, they noticed, were ever straying
As if impatient to be playing
Upon this pipe, as low it dangled
Over his vesture so old-fangled.)
"Yet," said he, "poor piper as I am,
In Tartary I freed the Cham,

Last June, from his huge swarms of gnats;
I eased in Asia the Nizam
Of a monstrous brood of vampyre-bats:
And as for what your brain bewilders,
If I can rid your town of rats
Will you give me a thousand guilders?"
"One? fifty thousand!" – was the exclamation
Of the astonished Mayor and Corporation.

Into the street the Piper stept,
Smiling first a little smile,
As if he knew what magic slept
In his quiet pipe the while;
Then, like a musical adept,
To blow the pipe his lips he wrinkled,
And green and blue his sharp eyes twinkled
Like a candle-flame where salt is sprinkled;
And ere three shrill notes the pipe uttered,
You heard as if an army muttered;
And the muttering grew to a grumbling;
And the grumbling grew to a mighty rumbling;
And out of the houses the rats came tumbling.
Great rats, small rats, lean rats, brawny rats,
Brown rats, black rats, grey rats, tawny rats,

Grave old plodders, gay young friskers,
Fathers, mothers, uncles, cousins,
Cocking tails and pricking whiskers,
Families by tens and dozens,
Brothers, sisters, husbands, wives —
Followed the Piper for their lives.
From street to street he piped advancing,
And step for step they followed dancing,
Until they came to the river Weser
Wherein all plunged and perished!
— Save one who, stout as Julius Cæsar,
Swam across and lived to carry
(As he, the manuscript he cherished)
To Rat-land home his commentáry:
Which was, "At the first shrill notes of the pipe,
I heard a sound as of scraping tripe,
And putting apples, wondrous ripe,
Into a cider-press's gripe:
And a moving away of pickle-tub boards,
And a leaving ajar of cónserve-cupboards,
And a drawing the corks of train-oil flasks,
And a breaking the hoops of butter-casks;
And it seemed as if a voice
(Sweeter far than by harp or by psaltery

Is breathed) called out, Oh rats, rejoice!
The world is grown to one vast dry-saltery!
So, munch on, crunch on, take your nuncheon,
Breakfast, supper, dinner, luncheon!
And just as a bulky sugar-puncheon,
All ready staved, like a great sun shone
Glorious scarce an inch before me,
Just as methought it said, Come, bore me!
— I found the Weser rolling o'er me."

You should have heard the Hamelin people
Ringing the bells till they rocked the steeple.
"Go," cried the Mayor, "and get long poles!
Poke out the nests and block up the holes!
Consult with carpenters and builders,
And leave in our town not even a trace
Of the rats!" — when suddenly, up the face
Of the Piper perked in the market-place,
With a "First, if you please, my thousand guilders!"

A thousand guilders! The Mayor looked blue;
So did the Corporation too.
For council dinners made rare havoc
With Claret, Moselle, Vin-de-Grave, Hock;
And half the money would replenish

Their cellar's biggest butt with Rhenish.
To pay this sum to a wandering fellow
With a gipsy coat of red and yellow!
"Beside," quoth the Mayor with a knowing wink,
"Our business was done at the river's brink;
We saw with our eyes the vermin sink,
And what's dead can't come to life, I think.
So, friend, we're not the folks to shrink
From the duty of giving you something to drink,
And a matter of money to put in your poke;
But as for the guilders, what we spoke
Of them, as you very well know, was in joke.
Besides, our losses have made us thrifty.
A thousand guilders! Come, take fifty!"

The Piper's face fell, and he cried,
"No trifling! I can't wait. Beside,
I've promised to visit by dinner time
Bagdad, and accept the prime
Of the Head-Cook's pottage, all he's rich in,
For having left, in the Caliph's kitchen,
Of a nest of scorpions no survivor –
With him I proved no bargain-driver,
With you, don't think I'll bate a stiver!

And folks who put me in a passion
May find me pipe to another fashion."

"How?" cried the Mayor, "d'ye think I'll brook
Being worse treated than a Cook?
Insulted by a lazy ribald
With idle pipe and vesture piebald?
You threaten us, fellow? Do your worst,
Blow your pipe there till you burst!"

Once more he stept into the street;
And to his lips again
Laid his long pipe of smooth straight cane;
And ere he blew three notes (such sweet
Soft notes as yet musician's cunning
Never gave the enraptured air)
There was a rustling, that seemed like a bustling
Of merry crowd justling at pitching and hustling,
Small feet were pattering, wooden shoes clattering,
Little hands clapping and little tongues chattering,
And, like fowls in a farm-yard when barley is scattering,
Out came the children running.
All the little boys and girls,
With rosy cheeks and flaxen curls,
And sparkling eyes and teeth like pearls,

Tripping and skipping, ran merrily after
The wonderful music with shouting and laughter.

The Mayor was dumb, and the Council stood
As if they were changed into blocks of wood,
Unable to move a step, or cry
To the children merrily skipping by –
And could only follow with the eye
That joyous crowd at the Piper's back.
But how the Mayor was on the rack,
And the wretched Council's bosoms beat,
As the Piper turned from the High Street
To where the Weser rolled its waters
Right in the way of their sons and daughters!
However he turned from South to West,
And to Koppelberg Hill his steps addressed,
And after him the children pressed;
Great was the joy in every breast.
"He never can cross that mighty top!
He's forced to let the piping drop,
And we shall see our children stop!"
When, lo, as they reached the mountain's side,
A wondrous portal opened wide,
As if a cavern was suddenly hollowed;

And the Piper advanced and the children followed,
And when all were in to the very last,
The door in the mountain-side shut fast.
Did I say, all? No! One was lame,
And could not dance the whole of the way;
And in after years, if you would blame
His sadness, he was used to say, –
"It's dull in our town since my playmates left!
I can't forget that I'm bereft
Of all the pleasant sights they see,
Which the Piper also promised me.
For he led us, he said, to a joyous land,
Joining the town and just at hand,
Where waters gushed and fruit-trees grew,
And flowers put forth a fairer hue,
And everything was strange and new;
The sparrows were brighter than peacocks here,
And their dogs outran our fallow deer,
And honey-bees had lost their stings,
And horses were born with eagles' wings:
And just as I became assured
My lame foot would be speedily cured,
The music stopped and I stood still,
And found myself outside the Hill,

Left alone against my will,
To go now limping as before,
And never hear of that country more!"

Alas, alas for Hamelin!
There came into many a burgher's pate
A text which says, that Heaven's Gate
Opes to the Rich at as easy rate
As the needle's eye takes a camel in!
The Mayor sent East, West, North and South,
To offer the Piper, by word of mouth,
Wherever it was men's lot to find him,
Silver and gold to his heart's content,
If he'd only return the way he went,
And bring the children behind him.
But when they saw 'twas a lost endeavour,
And Piper and dancers were gone for ever,
They made a decree that lawyers never
Should think their records dated duly
If, after the day of the month and year,
These words did not as well appear,
"And so long after what happened here
On the Twenty-second of July,
Thirteen-hundred and seventy-six":

And the better in memory to fix
The place of the children's last retreat,
They called it, the Pied Piper's Street —
Where any one playing on pipe or tabor
Was sure for the future to lose his labour
Nor suffered they hostelry or tavern
To shock with mirth a street so solemn;
But opposite the place of the cavern
They wrote the story on a column,
And on the great Church-Window painted
The same, to make the world acquainted
How their children were stolen away;
And there it stands to this very day.
And I must not omit to say
That in Transylvania there's a tribe
Of alien people that ascribe
The outlandish ways and dress
On which their neighbours lay such stress
To their fathers and mothers having risen
Out of some subterraneous prison
Into which they were trepanned
Long time ago in a mighty band
Out of Hamelin town in Brunswick land,
But how or why, they don't understand.

Sir Walter Scott

Bonny Dundee

To the Lords of Convention 'twas Claver'se who spoke,
"Ere the King's crown shall fall there are crowns to be
    broke;
So let each Cavalier who loves honour and me,
Come follow the bonnet of Bonny Dundee.

    "Come fill up my cup, come fill up my can,
    Come saddle your horses, and call up your men;
    Come open the West Port, and let me gang free,
    And it's room for the bonnets of Bonny Dundee!"

Dundee he is mounted, he rides up the street,
The bells are rung backward, the drums they are beat;
But the Provost, douce man, said, "Just e'en let him be,
The Gude Town is weel quit of that Deil of Dundee."

As he rode down the sanctified bends of the Bow,
Each carline was flyting and shaking her pow;
But the young plants of grace they look'd couthie and slee,
Thinking, "Luck to thy bonnet, thou Bonny Dundee!"

With sour-featured Whigs the Grassmarket was cramm'd
As if half the West had set tryst to be hang'd;
There was spite in each look, there was fear in each e'e,
As they watch'd for the bonnets of Bonny Dundee.

These cowls of Kilmarnock had spits and had spears,
And lang-hafted gullies to kill Cavaliers;
But they shrunk to close-heads, and the causeway was
    free,
At the toss of the bonnet of Bonny Dundee.

He spurr'd to the foot of the proud Castle rock,
And with the gay Gordon he gallantly spoke;
"Let Mons Meg and her marrows speak twa words or
    three,
For the love of the bonnet of Bonny Dundee."

The Gordon demands of him which way he goes –
"Where'er shall direct me the shade of Montrose!
Your Grace in short space shall hear tidings of me,
Or that low lies the bonnet of Bonny Dundee.

"There are hills beyond Pentland, and lands beyond
    Forth,
If there's lords in the Lowlands, there's chiefs in the
    North;
There are wild Duniewassals, three thousand times
    three,
Will cry hoigh! for the bonnet of Bonny Dundee.

"There's brass on the target of barken'd bull-hide;
There's steel in the scabbard that dangles beside;
The brass shall be burnish'd, the steel shall flash free,
At a toss of the bonnet of Bonny Dundee.

"Away to the hills, to the caves, to the rocks –
Ere I own an usurper, I'll couch with the fox;
And tremble, false Whigs, in the midst of your glee,
You have not seen the last of my bonnet and me!"

He waved his proud hand, and the trumpets were blown,
The kettle-drums clash'd, and the horsemen rode on,
Till on Ravelston's cliffs and on Clermiston's lee,
Died away the wild war-notes of Bonny Dundee.

   Come fill up my cup, come fill up my can,
   Come saddle the horses and call up the men,
   Come open your gates, and let me gae free,
   For it's up with the bonnets of Bonny Dundee!

ROBERT BURNS

MY HEART'S IN THE HIGHLANDS

My heart's in the Highlands, my heart is not here;
My heart's in the Highlands a-chasing the deer;
Chasing the wild deer, and following the roe,
My heart's in the Highlands, wherever I go.
Farewell to the Highlands, farewell to the North,
The birth-place of valour, the country of worth;
Wherever I wander, wherever I rove,
The hills of the Highlands for ever I love.

Farewell to the mountains, high cover'd with snow;
Farewell to the straths and green valleys below;
Farewell to the forests and wild-hanging woods;
Farewell to the torrents and loud-pouring floods.
My heart's in the Highlands, my heart is not here;
My heart's in the Highlands a-chasing the deer;
Chasing the wild deer, and following the roe,
My heart's in the Highlands, wherever I go.

CHRISTINA ROSSETTI

UPHILL

Does the road wind uphill all the way?
  Yes, to the very end.
Will the day's journey take the whole long day?
  From morn to night, my friend.

But is there for the night a resting-place?
  A roof for when the slow, dark hours begin.
May not the darkness hide it from my face?
  You cannot miss that inn.

Shall I meet other wayfarers at night?
  Those who have gone before.
Then must I knock, or call when just in sight?
  They will not keep you waiting at that door.

Shall I find comfort, travel-sore and weak?
  Of labour you shall find the sum.
Will there be beds for me and all who seek?
  Yea, beds for all who come.

CHARLES WOLFE

THE BURIAL OF SIR JOHN MOORE
AFTER CORUNNA

Not a drum was heard, not a funeral note,
As his corse to the rampart we hurried;
Not a soldier discharged his farewell shot
O'er the grave where our hero we buried.

We buried him darkly at dead of night,
The sods with our bayonets turning;
By the struggling moonbeam's misty light,
And the lantern dimly burning.

No useless coffin enclosed his breast,
Not in sheet or in shroud we wound him;
But he lay like a warrior taking his rest,
With his martial cloak around him.

Few and short were the prayers we said,
And we spoke not a word of sorrow;
But we steadfastly gazed on the face that was dead,
And we bitterly thought of the morrow.

We thought, as we hollowed his narrow bed,
And smoothed down his lonely pillow,
That the foe and the stranger would tread o'er his head,
And we far away on the billow!

Lightly they'll talk of the spirit that's gone,
And o'er his cold ashes upbraid him, –
But little he'll reck, if they let him sleep on
In the grave where a Briton has laid him.

But half of our heavy task was done
When the clock struck the hour for retiring;
And we heard the distant and random gun
That the foe was sullenly firing.

Slowly and sadly we laid him down,
From the field of his fame fresh and gory;
We carved not a line, and we raised not a stone –
But we left him alone with his glory.

ALICE MEYNELL

CHIMES

Brief, on a flying night
From the shaken tower,
A flock of bells take flight,
And go with the hour.

Like birds from the cote to the gales,
Abrupt – O hark!
A fleet of bells set sails,
And go to the dark.

Sudden the cold airs swing.
Alone, aloud,
A verse of bells takes wing
And flies with the cloud.

Rudyard Kipling

Eddi's Service

Eddi, priest of St Wilfrid
In his chapel at Manhood End,
Ordered a midnight service
For such as cared to attend.

But the Saxons were keeping Christmas,
And the night was stormy as well.
Nobody came to service,
Though Eddi rang the bell.

"'Wicked weather for walking,"
Said Eddi of Manhood End.
"But I must go on with the service
For such as care to attend."

The altar-lamps were lighted, –
An old marsh-donkey came,
Bold as a guest invited,
And stared at the guttering flame.

The storm beat on at the windows,
The water splashed on the floor,
And a wet, yoke-weary bullock
Pushed in through the open door.

"How do I know what is greatest,
How do I know what is least?
That is My Father's business,"
Said Eddi, Wilfrid's priest.

"But – three are gathered together –
Listen to me and attend.
I bring good news, my brethren!"
Said Eddi of Manhood End.

And he told the Ox of a Manger
And a Stall in Bethlehem,
And he spoke to the Ass of a Rider
That rode to Jerusalem.

They steamed and dripped in the chancel,
They listened and never stirred,
While, just as though they were Bishops,
Eddi preached them The Word,

Till the gale blew off on the marshes
And the windows showed the day,
And the Ox and the Ass together
Wheeled and clattered away.

And when the Saxons mocked him,
Said Eddi of Manhood End,
"I dare not shut His chapel
On such as care to attend."

ANDREW MARVELL

A DROP OF DEW

See how the orient dew
Shed from the bosom of the morn
   Into the blowing roses,
Yet careless of its mansion new,
For the clear region where 'twas born,
   Round it itself encloses;
And in its little globe's extent
Frames as it can its native element,
   How it the purple flower does slight,
Scarce touching where it lies!
But, gazing back upon the skies,
   Shines with a mournful light . . . .

Anonymous

Sir Patrick Spens

I The Sailing

The king sits in Dunfermline town
Drinking the blude-red wine;
"O where will I get a skeely skipper
To sail this new ship o' mine?"

O up and spake an eldern knight,
Sat at the king's right knee:
"Sir Patrick Spens is the best sailor
That ever sail'd the sea."

Our king has written a broad letter,
And seal'd it with his hand,
And sent it to Sir Patrick Spens,
Was walking on the strand.

"To Noroway, to Noroway,
To Noroway o'er the foam;
The king's daughter o' Noroway,
'Tis thou must bring her home."

The first word that Sir Patrick read
So loud, loud laugh'd he;
The next word that Sir Patrick read
The tear blinded his e'e.

"O who is this has done this deed
And told the king o' me,
To send us out, at this time o' year,
To sail upon the sea?

"Be it wind, be it wet, be it hail, be it sleet,
Our ship must sail the foam;
The king's daughter o' Noroway,
'Tis we must fetch her home."

They hoisted their sails on Monenday morn
With all the speed they may;
They have landed in Noroway
Upon a Wednesday.

II THE RETURN

The men of Norway seem to have insulted their
Scottish guests by hinting that they were staying too
long, and this caused Sir Patrick Spens to sail for
home without waiting for fair weather

"Make ready, make ready, my merry men all!
Our good ship sails the morn" –
"Now ever alack, my master dear,
I fear a deadly storm.

"I saw the new moon late yest'r-e'en
With the old moon in her arm;
And if we go to sea, master,
I fear we'll come to harm."

They had not sail'd a league, a league,
A league but barely three,
When the lift grew dark, and the wind blew loud,
And gurly grew the sea.

The anchors brake, and the topmast lap,
It was such a deadly storm;
And the waves came o'er the broken ship
Till all her sides were torn.

"O where will I get a good sailor
To take my helm in hand,
While I go up to the tall topmast
To see if I can spy land?" –

"O here am I, a sailor good,
To take the helm in hand,
While you go up to the tall topmast,
But I fear you'll ne'er spy land."

He had not gone a step, a step,
A step but barely one,
When a bolt flew out of our goodly ship,
And the salt sea it came in.

"Go fetch a web o' the silken cloth,
  Another o' the twine,
And wap them into our ship's side,
  And let not the sea come in."

They fetch'd a web o' the silken cloth,
  Another o' the twine,
And they wapp'd them round that good ship's side,
  But still the sea came in.

O loth, loth were our good Scots lords
  To wet their cork-heel'd shoon;
But long ere all the play was play'd
  They wet their hats aboon.

And many was the feather bed
  That flatter'd on the foam;
And many was the good lord's son
  That never more came home.

O long, long may the ladies sit,
With their fans into their hand,
Before they see Sir Patrick Spens
Come sailing to the strand!

And long, long may the maidens sit
With their gold combs in their hair,
A-waiting for their own dear loves!
For them they'll see no more.

Half-o'er, half-o'er to Aberdour,
'Tis fifty fathoms deep;
And there lies good Sir Patrick Spens,
With the Scots lords at his feet!

MATTHEW ARNOLD

DOVER BEACH

The sea is calm to-night.
The tide is full, the moon lies fair
Upon the straits; — on the French coast the light
Gleams and is gone; the cliffs of England stand,
Glimmering and vast, out in the tranquil bay.
Come to the window, sweet is the night-air!
Only, from the long line of spray
Where the sea meets the moon-blanch'd land,
Listen! you hear the grating roar
Of pebbles which the waves draw back, and fling,
At their return, up the high strand,
Begin, and cease, and then again begin,
With tremulous cadence slow, and bring
The eternal note of sadness in.

Sophocles long ago
Heard it on the Aegean, and it brought
Into his mind the turbid ebb and flow
Of human misery; we
Find also in the sound a thought,
Hearing it by this distant northern sea.

The Sea of Faith
Was once, too, at the full, and round earth's shore
Lay like the folds of a bright girdle furl'd.
But now I only hear
Its melancholy, long, withdrawing roar,
Retreating, to the breath
Of the night-wind, down the vast edges drear
And naked shingles of the world.

Ah, love, let us be true
To one another! for the world, which seems
To lie before us like a land of dreams,
So various, so beautiful, so new,
Hath really neither joy, nor love, nor light,
Nor certitude, nor peace, nor help for pain;
And we are here as on a darkling plain
Swept with confused alarms of struggle and flight,
Where ignorant armies clash by night.

WILLIAM WORDSWORTH

DAFFODILS

I wander'd lonely as a cloud
  That floats on high o'er vales and hills,
When all at once I saw a crowd,
  A host, of golden daffodils;
Beside the lake, beneath the trees,
Fluttering and dancing in the breeze.

Continuous as the stars that shine
  And twinkle on the Milky Way,
They stretch'd in never-ending line
  Along the margin of a bay:
Ten thousand saw I at a glance,
Tossing their heads in sprightly dance.

The waves beside them danced, but they
  Out-did the sparkling waves in glee:
A poet could not but be gay,
  In such a jocund company:
I gazed – and gazed – but little thought
What wealth the show to me had brought:

For oft, when on my couch I lie
    In vacant or in pensive mood,
They flash upon that inward eye
    Which is the bliss of solitude;
And then my heart with pleasure fills,
And dances with the daffodils.

JOHN KEATS

TO AUTUMN

Season of mists and mellow fruitfulness!
  Close bosom-friend of the maturing sun;
Conspiring with him how to load and bless
  With fruit the vines that round the thatch-eaves run;
To bend with apples the moss'd cottage-trees,
  And fill all fruit with ripeness to the core;
    To swell the gourd, and plump the hazel shells
  With a sweet kernel; to set budding more,
And still more, later flowers for the bees,
Until they think warm days will never cease,
  For Summer has o'er-brimm'd their clammy cells.

Who hath not seen thee oft amid thy store?
  Sometimes whoever seeks abroad may find
Thee sitting careless on a granary floor,
  Thy hair soft-lifted by the winnowing wind
Or on a half-reap'd furrow sound asleep,
  Drowsed with the fume of poppies, while thy hook
    Spares the next swath and all its twinèd flowers;
And sometimes like a gleaner thou dost keep

Steady thy laden head across a brook;
  Or by a cider-press, with patient look,
    Thou watchest the last oozings hours by hours.

Where are the songs of Spring? Ay, where are they?
  Think not of them, thou hast thy music too, –
While barrèd clouds bloom the soft-dying day,
  And touch the stubble-plains with rosy hue;
Then in a wailful choir the small gnats mourn
  Among the river sallows, borne aloft
    Or sinking as the light wind lives or dies;
And full-grown lambs loud bleat from hilly bourn;
  Hedge-crickets sing; and now with treble soft
  The redbreast whistles from a garden-croft;
    And gathering swallows twitter in the skies.